EXPIRY DATE

EXPIRY DATE

Raewyn Caisley

Nelson
an International Thomson Publishing company I(T)P®

Melbourne • Albany, NY • Belmont, CA • Bonn • Boston • Cincinnati
Detroit • Johannesburg • London • Madrid • Mexico City • New York
Paris • Singapore • Tokyo • Toronto • Washington

Nelson I T P®
102 Dodds Street
South Melbourne 3205

Email nelsonitp@nelson.com.au
Website http://www.nelsonitp.com

Nelson I T P® *an International Thomson Publishing company*

First published in 1998
10 9 8 7 6 5 4
05 04 03 02 01 00 99
Copyright © Nelson ITP 1999

COPYRIGHT
Apart from fair dealing for the purposes of study, research, criticism or review, or as permitted under Part VB of the Copyright Act, no part of this book may be reproduced by any process without permission. Copyright owners may take legal action against a person who infringes on their copyright through unauthorised copying. Enquiries should be directed to the publisher.

National Library of Australia
Cataloguing-in-Publication data

Raewyn Caisley
 Expiry date.
 ISBN 0 17 009434 0
 ISBN 0 17 009414 6 (set).
 I. Title. (Series: BlitzIt).
 A823.3

Editorial production by BDP
Designed by Christine Deering
Illustrations by Grant Adam/Uncommon Characters
Cover designed by Grant Adam/Uncommon Characters
Text designed by Christine Deering
Typeset in Clearface Regular
Printed in Singapore by Kin Keong Printing Co. Pte. Ltd

Nelson Australia Pty Limited ACN 058 280 149 (incorporated in Victoria) trading as Nelson ITP.

Contents

Chapter	1	Richard Corelli's Expiry Date	3
Chapter	2	The Gardener Appears	8
Chapter	3	Welcome to My Nightmare	13
Chapter	4	Supermarket Sweep	16
Chapter	5	Branded!	22
Chapter	6	Freak-out!	26
Chapter	7	The Day Before	32
Chapter	8	Doctor Schrinkentwist	36
Chapter	9	Thirtieth of June	39
Chapter	10	Just Desserts	44

You know how there's always one kid in the class who gets teased to death? Well, in our class the kid's name was Richard Corelli and we all teased Richard because he was fat. I mean really fat. Inner-tube around his stomach and seven chins fat... but maybe I shouldn't have put it like that...

I don't mean I shouldn't have told you how fat he was. What I mean is, maybe I shouldn't have said that we teased Richard TO DEATH.

Chapter 1

Richard Corelli's Expiry Date

It all began the day we came up with the ultimate tease. The one that would get us into the *Guinness Book of Records* for the most inspired piece of cruelty to another human being.

On a scale of 1 to 10 this was an 11. Quentin Marshall, King of Cruel, came up with the idea. Bradley, the brown nose, egged him on as usual. But I was the one who added the touch that made it an 11.

No-one in the class spared a thought for

our victim. We didn't stop to think how we were making Richard feel. Except maybe Quentin, who enjoys inflicting pain.

He's the type who sticks pins into nice plump spiders, then pulls off their legs. Anyway here's how it went...

We'd been working on a project at school about food – how it's made and packaged. Miss Wong had been talking about expiry dates on processed food, and how they help us to avoid eating stuff that has gone off.

When she'd finished, Miss Wong left the room to collect something from the staff room. We were meant to be working in groups, discussing the project. As usual, however, when the conversation turned to food, our thoughts turned to Richard.

"You like your food, Richo. How about this – 30:06:99. That's your own personal expiry date." said Quentin. "That's the day all your clogged-up arteries shut down completely, and the blood supply to your heart dries up forever – and – your – poor – fatty – heart – stops!"

Quentin was going for an Oscar; grabbing at his chest and staggering around. Richard, as usual, was just sitting there, looking like a scared rabbit. He never dared to say anything to Quentin.

I was busy too, putting the finishing touches to my artwork. I had cut a piece from a sheet of art paper, just the right size to wrap around my pencil jar. It looked like the label on a glass jar from the supermarket.

On the "label" I'd drawn a picture. It was of dozens of fat, juicy, pickled Richards, their faces and palms squashed up against the glass. They reminded me of those pickled people you see at craft fairs. You know, the ones stuffed into jars and made of old pantyhose and cotton wool. Anyway, I thought it looked cool.

For the finishing touch I took Quentin's fluoro purple marker and wrote "EXP. DATE:

30:06:99" across the bottom in dot-matrix printing, like you'd find on a real jar of pickles. Then I went to grab a bit of sticky-tape off Miss Wong's desk.

Quentin, meanwhile, had finally "died" on Richard's desk, and Richard's eyes were popping right out of his head. Quentin opened one eye as I passed, and when he saw Richard's face he started to laugh. He jumped up and ran to the blackboard.

He picked up some white chalk and started writing across the top of the board, where Miss Wong usually writes the date. In big, spooky letters, he wrote: *30th June, 1999.* Then he picked up a red chalk and added great globules of blood that dripped from the date. The class was in uproar, running around all over the place.

"Look out, you guys, she's coming," Bradley Blakehurst yelled, and everybody dashed back to their desks.

Richard Corelli's Expiry Date

Quentin rubbed off the blood from under the date. He was just sitting down again when Miss Wong walked in.

Chapter 2

The Gardener Appears

"Hello, again, 6W," she said.

"Hello, Miss Wong," everyone chanted. Everyone, that is, except Richard. He was staring, bug-eyed, at the date.

The whole class went silent. Miss Wong looked at us.

"Did I miss something?" she asked. "I don't like it when you're so quiet. It makes me think that you've been up to something. Is that right?"

"No, Miss," giggled Bradley.

Miss Wong turned to the blackboard and Bradley dissolved.

"Who wrote the date on the blackboard?" she asked. "Whoever it was got it wrong. The thirtieth of June isn't until next week."

Miss Wong turned around. She looked at Richard.

"Richard, will you rub it off for me?" she asked, handing him the duster.

Richard's face turned white under his pudgy red cheeks. Then he started to cry. Big, blocked-up, snot-sobs, like he couldn't breathe.

Bradley lay his head down on his arms. His back shook like he was crying too, but everyone knew he was just giggling.

Quentin Marshall leaned back in his chair, grinning. He looked very pleased with his morning's work.

"I think I'd like to see Richard and Bradley in the corridor," said Miss Wong. "You too, Quentin."

Nobody said anything as they walked out of the room, but as soon as the door closed I tiptoed over and swapped my pencil jar with Richard's.

Now, I can't say I was expecting a round of applause or anything, but I thought that someone would at least want to check out my drawing. But there was nothing, just a horrible silence.

I looked at everyone's faces and they stared right back at me, as if I'd done something very un-funny. I felt as though I was walking through the supermarket in my pyjamas.

Then it dawned on me that they weren't staring at me so much as *behind* me, and my embarrassed feeling became a creepy "there's-someone-standing-right-behind-you" feeling. I spun around – and there was.

Outside the classroom window was a man, standing perfectly still – *and he was staring right at me!* In his left hand he held a garden

The Gardener Appears

rake, which made me think that he might be the new school gardener. The last gardener had left at the end of term.

The man's face was dark and dirty and he was wearing a mouldy, moth-eaten, black woollen beanie pulled all the way down over his ears. Anyway, he kept staring at me for what felt like hours, and frowning. He reminded me of one of those creepy paintings in horror movies, with holes cut so you can see the eyes move – he was completely still, but looked intently at my pencil jar on Richard's desk, at the date Quentin had written on the board, and then back at me, all without moving his head.

The door opened then, and the others came back in and sat down. Miss Wong smiled at Richard and patted his shoulder. Quentin pretended to stick his finger down his throat. I hardly noticed. I was in shock.

"Sit down please, Andrew Short," said Miss

Wong and that's when I realised I'd just been standing there like a zombie, staring out the window.

I quickly went and sat at my desk. When I looked back at the window again, the "gardener" had gone. I was left with a sick feeling that somehow wouldn't go. Whoever he was, he chilled me to the bone.

Chapter 3

Welcome to My Nightmare

That was how the most terrible week of my life started. I had no idea, then, how it was going to end.

The gardener guy spooked me. I kept thinking I was seeing him. He was on the far side of the playground at recess. Behind one of the infant's classrooms when we were having assembly. And in the canteen at lunch time.

The funny thing was that I didn't know *why* I was worried. I just had this weird feeling of doom. A heaviness, like I'd done something I shouldn't have, and now it was too late to turn the clock back. It *might* have had something to do with Richard, but I didn't want to think too much about him. It would have only made me feel worse. My life was quickly becoming a nightmare. Meanwhile everyone else kept paying out on Richard as normal. I still joined in the teasing as well, even though I didn't have my usual enthusiasm.

On Wednesday afternoon we were playing softball on the back oval. Richard, as usual, had been last to be picked. Sport was always bad for him, because he was self-conscious about his weight.

When he finally managed to connect bat to ball and ran for first base, I ran behind him, my knuckles dragging in the dirt. Kids on both teams were doubled-up laughing, but then I stopped dead. I was sure I could see the creepy gardener again, watching me from over near the Art Department. Suddenly, playing ape didn't seem very funny.

I told myself that I hadn't stopped because I was feeling guilty or anything; I was just freaked out by the gardener. Whatever the reason, Quentin wasn't impressed with me. When the bell rang he said I'd gone soft.

Chapter 4

Supermarket Sweep

Nan picked me up after school that day. Mum had told Nan I would help her with her shopping. After my experience on the oval, it was the last thing I felt like doing. I didn't even say "Hi" when I met her at the front gate. I just said, "Come on, Nan," and walked off down the street.

Quentin flashed past us on his bike, grinning.

When we got to the supermarket, Nan sent

me off to find things for her. "We could have hamburgers for dinner," she said.

They might sound all right to you, but they weren't your average hamburgers. Nan made them with canned meat. She said it "served the boys well in the Great War". So off I went to find a can of Spam, to make pension burgers.

"Get the Home Label, Andrew," Nan called after me. "And don't forget to check the expiry date. Thelma Lewis had a terrible experience last week with a can of sardines."

Nan reckoned Home Label meant cheap-but-a-day-before-rotten, so I always had to check the expiry date. I was staring at the shelves and shelves full of canned, processed meat (possibly a day off being rotten), when I looked up... and there he was!

It was the gardener again! I couldn't believe it. He must have been following me. I felt sick, and grabbed some Home Label ham off the shelf, hoping to make a quick escape. Then the gardener disappeared around a shelf, and an empty shopping trolley rolled into view, *all by itself!* It rolled squeakily into the middle of the canned-meat aisle, and stopped dead.

I turned to run when an earthy odour filled my nostrils. I looked up, and he was there again! He was only about ten or fifteen metres away... and this time I could smell him.

A damp, musty, smell wafted from his clothes, a bit like compost. I guess it was the sort of smell you'd expect from a gardener, but six times as strong. Like he'd actually been *under* the dirt, not digging in it. He smelled like he'd been underground for twenty years.

The gardener wandered over to a shelf of spaghetti sauce and casually picked up a jar. He looked at it closely, turned it around, and checked the seal on the lid. Then, in slow motion, he dropped it into the trolley and looked at me. And I mean straight at me. No polite glances or anything. He stared directly into my eyes ... and something changed. You know what it's like when you're watching a film and there's a bad bit of editing? Something flicks. You know it's happened, but then it's gone.

I felt the weight of the can of ham in my hand. I studied it as the guy passed behind me with his trolley and his single jar of spaghetti sauce. His smell slipped by me like a gas leak.

Then my eyes focused on the top of the canned ham and there it was: EXP. DATE: 30:06:99. In purple dot-matrix printing. The real thing.

I dropped the can as if it was hot and took a step back, bumping into a woman behind me.

The lady frowned at me. Then she looked down at the jar of peanut butter she was holding. "Thirtieth of June," she mumbled to herself. "Must be why it's on special." She put the jar into her trolley and walked off.

I grabbed a jar of peanut butter from the shelf and it was the same! EXP. DATE: 30:06:99. I grabbed jar after jar and they all had the same date. Even the brands that weren't on special. I stopped plundering the peanut butter and looked up and down the aisle…and then I started to run.

I ran from one item to the next, checking everything – and each item I looked at was the same.

Cannelloni – EXP. DATE: 30:06:99. Baked beans – EXP. DATE: 30:06:99. Button mushrooms – EXP. DATE: 30:06:99. Black olives ... baby sweet corn ... butterscotch steamed pudding – EXP. DATE: 30:06:99. The bread, the cheese, the eggs, even the stuff in the fridges. Everything had the same date stamped on it.

I stood beside the frozen goods, panting.

"What's the matter with you, boy?" asked Nan, behind me. "And where's the Spam?"

"It's not right!" I yelled at her. "Everything's got the same expiry date on it. I can't work it out! I don't know what's happening!"

"Oh, pull yourself together, boy," said Nan,

shaking me by the jumper. "What are you on about? Go and get my Spam and we'll have a cup of tea in the coffee shop."

She tottered off toward the checkout. I stood there and watched her go – and there he was again, getting money out of his wallet to pay for the spaghetti sauce!

As soon as I saw him he looked up. It was as if we had some kind of psychic thing going. This time, those weird eyes of his stared straight into my soul. I saw them in every detail, like we were standing right in front of each other. Big, black pupils, like holes carved in his head, surrounded by muddy, browny, green irises; the whites with a sort of old-bone-yellow tinge to them; a network of veins spreading out from the middle...

Standing there, with those decaying-corpse eyes looking right through me, the thought crossed my mind that maybe the thirtieth of June wasn't Richard's expiry date. *Maybe it was MINE!*

Chapter 5

Branded!

Things got really, *really*, weird after that. I guess I might have been getting sick with fear, or maybe it was because I wasn't getting a lot of sleep.

I couldn't shut my eyes in bed without having nightmares. All of them were about the sinister gardener; but sometimes Richard was in them, or Quentin (the ones with him were particularly evil). Sometimes even my family appeared – Mum, Dad and Nan. Miss Wong turned up in the freakiest one of all.

• • •

In the dream, she'd been invited to dinner. Everyone was sitting at the table, then in walked the gardener with a big covered platter on a trolley. When he lifted the cover up, there I was. I was the main course.

"Yum, yum," said Richard. He picked up his fork, stuck it into my chest and started to eat.

"All right!" said Quentin. He sucked a bit of intestine out of my guts like spaghetti.

Nan put my big toe into a burger bun and Mum and Dad shared my fingers. Mum always liked the wings when we had a roast chicken. As she munched away I heard her say that I was very tasty, but that she would have preferred me marinated in plum sauce or honey soy.

Miss Wong asked the gardener to pluck out my eyeballs to make her some soup. As he leaned over me with a skewer I woke up in a sweat, screaming.

• • •

The next morning, after that dream, the most bizarre thing yet happened. I didn't notice it until I was brushing my teeth.

I was standing in front of the bathroom mirror, cleaning my teeth listlessly after another sleepless night. It was then that I noticed a purple mark on my forehead, right on the hairline. I stopped scrubbing and took my toothbrush out of my mouth.

Toothpaste ran from my open mouth in big, foamy globs when I saw what the mark was. EXPIRES 30 JUN 1999 – written in my own veins.

The veins were raised slightly and I could see my blood pumping through them. Blue blood. Starved of oxygen. Heading back to my heart.

I dropped my toothbrush and ran my finger over the mark to see whether it was real. It was. It felt warm beneath my fingers, and had a spongy, squishy texture. The veins were so close to the surface of my skin that I

I was scared that if I rubbed too hard they'd burst. My entire forehead was hot and inflamed, as if I'd been branded.

It was then that I fainted.

Chapter 6

Freak-out!

I stayed home from school for the rest of the week. It wasn't hard to convince Mum I was sick.

I phoned Quentin after school on the day that the date appeared, and blurted out everything that had happened to me. He just laughed, and told me to keep taking the medication.

I phoned Bradley next. Unbelievably, he thought I'd been incredibly cool and had myself tattooed. The jerk even asked where he could get the same thing done.

Then I phoned Richard. He sounded a bit shocked to be hearing from me.

"A–Andrew? What are you doing? I thought you were sick."

"I guess you could say that. Richard, has anything weird been happening? You haven't seen a strange guy hanging around? Or noticed anything else?"

"Nah, just the usual. Quentin throwing his weight around."

I said an embarrassed "Goodbye", and hung up quickly.

• • •

In a way I was relieved that Richard was okay but, then again, in another way I wasn't. It didn't make sense. *I* had a pulsating expiry date on my forehead, but nothing weird seemed to have happened to any of the others.

All I could come up with was that I was the only one in the room when the gardener turned up. I knew now that he was responsible. He was making everything happen. What I didn't know was where it was all heading.

After I'd phoned everybody, I couldn't think of anything else to do. I just lay down to wait, sort of like an animal that's been run over.

I stayed in bed most of the time for the next few days, curled up in a ball and staring blindly at the wall or at the ceiling. Once or twice Mum had to go out for something, and she refused to leave me at home by myself. "You're not yourself, dear. I think you should come."

This was how I came to have my freak-out at the bank.

• • •

I sat in the back of the car on the way, being really careful not to bump my head. I'd covered up the expiry date with a cap.

"Come on, Andrew," Mum said when we got to the mall. "This won't take long."

Freak-out!

So I got out of the car and followed her to the bank. I must have looked like I'd completely cracked. I walked behind her all hunched over, staring like a lunatic at people's faces as they passed.

Mum went and joined the queue in the bank and I sat in one of the chairs by the wall. I was sitting there, eyeballing everybody, when I heard a soft *click*.

Slowly, I looked behind me.

There on the wall, right over my head, was the calendar. And the date it was showing? You guessed it. The thirtieth of June!

I yelled out, "Ahhhh! There's something wrong with the calendar!" A teller gave me a funny look and came over and fiddled with it. Then he went back to the counter.

Click, it went again.

I jumped out of the chair and bumped into the table beside me. The bank slips spilled out all over the floor.

Expiry Date

Mum and the teller came running over. I tried to help them tidy up, but then I saw them. The withdrawal slips! The deposit slips were still all blank, but something, or someone, had filled in the date boxes on all the withdrawal slips – with the thirtieth of June! And underneath, on each one, they'd filled in my name!

I started riffling through the slips on the floor, checking them all. I must have looked like a real fool. Anyway, suddenly I realised what I was doing. I stopped and glanced up, still on my hands and knees, surrounded by paper. Everyone in the queue was staring at me, and so were the tellers.

There was only one person with their back to me, and that was the man at the front of the queue. He had a big, dirty, brown coat on and over the top of his turned-up collar I could just make out...a black beanie.

I started to sniff the air like a dog. Mum

Freak-out!

and the teller gently helped me to my feet and led me to the door.

Chapter 7

The Day Before

The next day was the twenty-ninth.

I struggled out of bed at dawn after another terrible night. If it wasn't the nightmares, it was the pain in my head, or the smell in my room keeping me awake. The smell of the gardener seemed to be everywhere.

My expiry date had grown more and more swollen. That night it had throbbed so much I could actually hear my own pulse, when I was awake and asleep.

The Day Before

I was kind-of groggy as I stumbled into the kitchen. I was also really hungry. I hadn't eaten for days.

The kitchen cupboard was open so I took out a can of cheesy spaghetti. I knew what would be there when I turned it over, so I wasn't surprised to see that the expiry date was the thirtieth of June. In a sort of half-awake dream, I went through the cupboard, knocking things over and making a mess. Everything, of course, had the thirtieth of June on it.

The fridge was the same. I took a swig from the milk carton and it had that too-sweet taste of milk about to go off. Of course, when I looked at the expiry date, I saw that it *was* about to go off.

I started to giggle, in a crazy sort of way, over the milk. A thin line of milk dribbled down my chin and dripped on to the floor. I didn't even stop to wipe it away.

I ran myself a nice, clean, fresh, glass of

Expiry Date

water from the tap and walked over to the kitchen window. The sun was just showing on the horizon. Not the golden orb, but the red glow that came before it.

I sipped the clear water. It tasted like life. Then I screamed and dropped the glass on the floor.

Standing there in my front garden, framed by the window, with the sun rising like a halo behind him, was the gardener.

Totally mesmerised, I watched him. With his free hand, (he was carrying his rake again), he drew a diagonal line in the air, as if he was crossing something out.

Our calendar hung on the wall by the window. Like a robot, I turned towards it. The last drop of milk dripped from my chin.

A purple dot appeared in the top left hand corner of one of the date squares. Then, all by itself, the line started to grow. When the day was crossed off I looked at the numbers. There

The Day Before

was a "23" in the top of the square. The twenty-third was the day the nightmare had begun.

One by one, the gardener crossed off the days. As he drew closer to the thirtieth, I started to lose it.

I was trembling by the twenty-fifth, really shaking by the twenty-seventh, and by the twenty-ninth I'd started to cry. Big, blocked-up snot-sobs, like someone else I knew. Richard.

Hysterical, I ran into Mum and Dad's room. I blubbered about Richard, and how sorry I was, and about Nan and the supermarket and expiry dates, and calendars, and dying, and, well, about *everything*.

Chapter 8

Dr Schrinkentwist

Mum and Dad were no help whatsoever. Neither was Nan who came tottering in for a breakfast cuppa. To give them their due, it was a pretty wild story I told them. I'm sure that if someone had told it to me, I wouldn't have known what to say, either.

Mum, Dad and Nan made a few soothing noises, then called the doctor. He came over and checked me out, and said there was nothing physically wrong. He seemed a bit baffled by the expiry date, though.

"It looks like there's a small blockage in one of the veins running behind the forehead. But given Andrew's age, that seems very unlikely. I think he's in a bit of a state about school, and that he should get some rest. Here's a medical certificate for the next week."

I spent the morning lying in Mum and Dad's bed, curled up in the foetal position. All I could do was rub at my mark, then tug at my hair to try to hide it. That stupid expiry date had become an obsession.

In the afternoon, Mum and Dad took me off to visit the "mental health" expert at the local bulk-billing medical centre. Old Doctor Schrinkentwist was so like a cartoon psychoanalyst it was almost a joke. His theory was that the forehead rubbing and hair tugging pointed to "a fault in the head", but he failed to offer any further advice.

In desperation, Dad phoned his sister, my Aunty Rose, who was doing a psychology degree at university. Aunty Rose came over for dinner, and, after talking to Mum and Dad, then me, she decided I had "issues to resolve", possibly with someone called Richard. (Aunty Rose reads tarot cards and spins bits of crystal as well, so I don't think my parents took her diagnosis too seriously.) Then she told them they should send me back to school!

• • •

So that's what happened. On the morning of the thirtieth of June, I found myself walking like a zombie to my bedroom, to collect my stuff for school.

I didn't tell anyone that once I'd stopped blubbering the previous day, lying there in Mum and Dad's bed, I'd realised I had to go back to school, too. It was like the flash of knowledge I'd had in the supermarket. Suddenly, I'd just known.

Whatever was going to happen to me was going to happen at school.

Chapter 9

Thirtieth of June

"Hey, Shortie," yelled Quentin from over at the taps. "They've let you out of your straitjacket!"

I kept walking.

When I reached the classroom I dropped my bag in the corridor and went and sat at my desk.

Slowly, the rest of the class started to drift in. I must have looked strange. Nobody came near me.

Bradley and Quentin had moved their desks closer together and they were cooking up something. I didn't even look at them. Richard's desk, between Miss Wong's and mine, was empty.

Then Miss Wong walked in.

"Well, hello, Andrew," she said. "I hope you're feeling better."

The expiry date on my forehead started to throb faintly. I couldn't say anything so I just nodded.

Quentin and Bradley passed a note down the row. On it they'd drawn a picture of a graveyard, and on one of the headstones they'd written: "RICHARD CORELLI – EXPIRED 30:06:99".

I looked at Quentin like he was a dead man. He sneered back at me. I grabbed a felt pen and wrote "GROW UP" on the note, in letters big enough for Quentin to see, then I held it up for him. I was past caring that Miss Wong might see me. Then I let the piece of paper fall to the floor, as Miss Wong turned around from the blackboard.

I looked at Richard's desk and my head throbbed a bit harder. I began to hear my own blood in my ears. Then I heard a crashing sound in the corridor. We all turned to the door... and Richard walked in.

"Quickly, please, Richard," Miss Wong said calmly.

He sat at his desk in front of me and I felt the expiry date on my head throb and double in size. *Swoosh swoosh, swoosh swoosh, swoosh swoosh*, it went as my blood pumped through it. All around me the world started to turn faintly red.

"Who can tell me what the date is today?" came Miss Wong's voice through the haze. "That's right, Bradley, the thirtieth of June."

I tried to focus on her.

"Andrew, would you write the date up for me?" she asked and held out the chalk.

Very slowly, as if I was 100-years-old, I got to my feet. Richard leaned over and picked up

Expiry Date

Quentin's note from the floor. He smiled shyly at me.

Like a guy on death row, I walked between the desks to the front of the room and took the chalk from Miss Wong.

Three, zero, dot, dot, I wrote.

My left knee went from under me. Miss Wong looked over. I held on to the rail.

Zero, six, dot, dot.

My arm shook uncontrollably. I could see wet finger marks on the chalk.

I turned around and looked at Richard and he smiled kindly at me.

Nine, nine, I wrote – and collapsed.

Miss Wong came rushing toward me and caught me as I fell. Everybody leaned over their desks so that they could see.

As I came to, I put my hand up to my head. There was nothing! No blood. No throbbing. My forehead was cool.

I grabbed a can of pencils, spilling them

Thirtieth of June

everywhere, and looked at my reflection in the side of the can. The expiry date had gone.

Then, in the background, I saw the tiny reflection of a man walking out the school gate.

Jumping to my feet I ran to the window, but whoever it was had gone.

"The gardener!" I yelled.

Miss Wong looked strangely at me, not sure what to do.

"Come over here, Andrew," she said very gently. "I think you need to sit down."

"But it was the gardener!" I yelled again.

"Andrew," she said. "I don't know why it seems to be so important to you, but the Principal hasn't hired anyone yet ... "

I stood there and stared disbelievingly out the front gate. Then, shaken, I turned to go back to my desk – just as Quentin Marshall leapt to his feet, made a sort of strangled gurgling sound, and grabbed at his chest...

Chapter 10

Just Desserts

During recess, Richard and I went over to see Quentin in sick-bay.

We snuck quietly past the Principal's office – and he was interviewing an old man. An old man with a navy blue fishing hat ... but that's another story.

When we got to the sick-bay, Quentin was curled up on the bed in the foetal position, moaning.

And you may not believe this, but Richard actually said something – to Quentin!

We both stuck our heads around the sick-bay door and Richard said, "Take it from me, Quentin, I'm an expert. You shouldn't have pinched those cream doughnuts from me yesterday and gutsed them all."

Quentin moaned and tried to throw a cushion at us. "It wasn't that, you dorks!" he said. "I know how many I ate."

"Oh, well," said Richard. "Maybe you're right. Maybe that wasn't it...maybe they were just past their expiry date!"

About the Author

Raewyn Caisley is the author of a number of books for children, including *Monkey Trix*, published by Penguin in 1997.
She lives in a beachside suburb of Sydney.

Blitz It

Hell-ectric Guitar
by Brian McGinn

Frank meets a mysterious old man who sells him a battered guitar. The guitar can make him a superstar – but what does it, and the old man, want in return? Will Frank last long enough to enjoy his fame?

Birthday Surprise
by Margaret Pearce

Freckles, Frazzle and James think they'll surprise their mother on her birthday with a plant they have grown themselves. The birthday plant however, shows a sinister appetite for food – and worse!

Blitz It

The Twins in the Trunk
by Susan Green

When Katie finds an old trunk in the cellar under her house, she thinks she's found bushranger's treasure. What she *has* found is ghost trouble – and double trouble at that!

Katie and Angus soon find that some things are better left unopened...

Monopillar
by Alan Horsfield

A weird alien mystery set in and around Sydney's Powerhouse Museum. Who are the mysterious scientists, and why are they carrying bags of bones around? And why is the Monorail looking so strange?

BlitzIt

***BlitzIt* is here! Once you've read one *BlitzIt* book, you'll want to read them all.**

Mystery ... adventure ... alien visitors ... weird science ... spooky happenings ... *BlitzIt* has something for everyone!

Bargains from Outer Space
by Heather Hammonds

Rod and Sean get more than they bargain for when they flick through the channels on the new TV. Who, or what, are the strange creatures selling fantastic gadgets? And do they really deliver? Find out what happens when Rod and Sean go on a shopping spree that is out-of-this-world!